NOTHING COOLER THAN A DINOSAUR

By CODY MCKINNEY

Illustrated by DAN CRISP

CANTATA
LEARNING

MANKATO, MINNESOTA

CANTATA LEARNING

MANKATO, MINNESOTA

Published by Cantata Learning
1710 Roe Crest Drive
North Mankato, MN 56003
www.cantatalearning.com

Library of Congress Control Number: 2014938332
ISBN: 978-1-63290-074-6

Nothing Cooler Than a Dinosaur by Cody McKinney
Illustrated by Dan Crisp

Book design by Tim Palin Creative
Music produced by Wes Schuck
Audio recorded, mixed, and mastered at Two Fish Studios, Mankato, MN

Printed in the United States of America.

VISIT

WWW.CANTATALEARNING.COM/ACCESS-OUR-MUSIC

Way back 200 million years or more,
they'd squeak and **squawk** and howl and roar.

They'd fly or walk on two legs, some on four.

They were the mighty, mighty dinosaurs.

There were tiny ones smaller than a mouse,
the really giant ones as big as a house.

Some had spikes and horns to use for their **protection**.

It helped them stick around awhile before the big
extinction of the dinosaurs.

The real mean ones were meat eaters. It helped to make them bigger.

Well others were plant eaters. I guess they watched their figure.

A group of them is called a **herd**, but many lived alone.

One thing they had in common was they're *bad to the bone*.

What happened to the dinosaurs? Why are they not around?

Perhaps a rock just hit the Earth and knocked them out of town.

Or maybe a volcano spilled some **lava** all around.

The truth of it is oftentimes these answers can't be found.

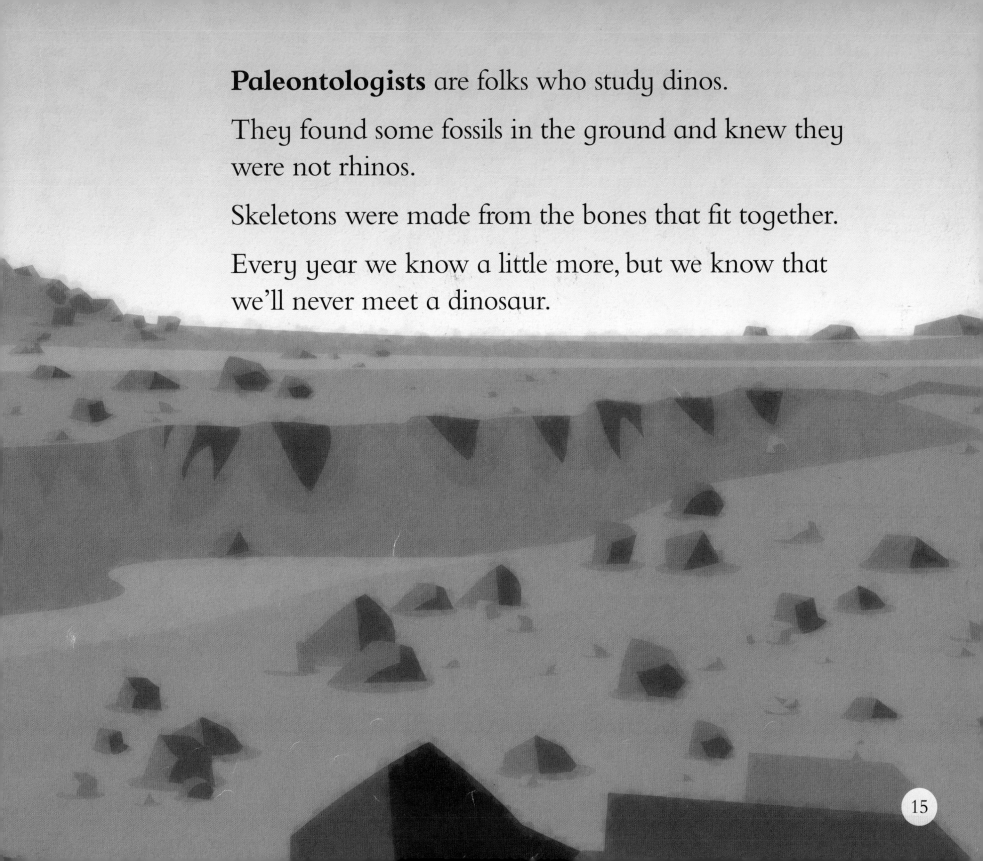

Paleontologists are folks who study dinos.

They found some fossils in the ground and knew they were not rhinos.

Skeletons were made from the bones that fit together.

Every year we know a little more, but we know that we'll never meet a dinosaur.

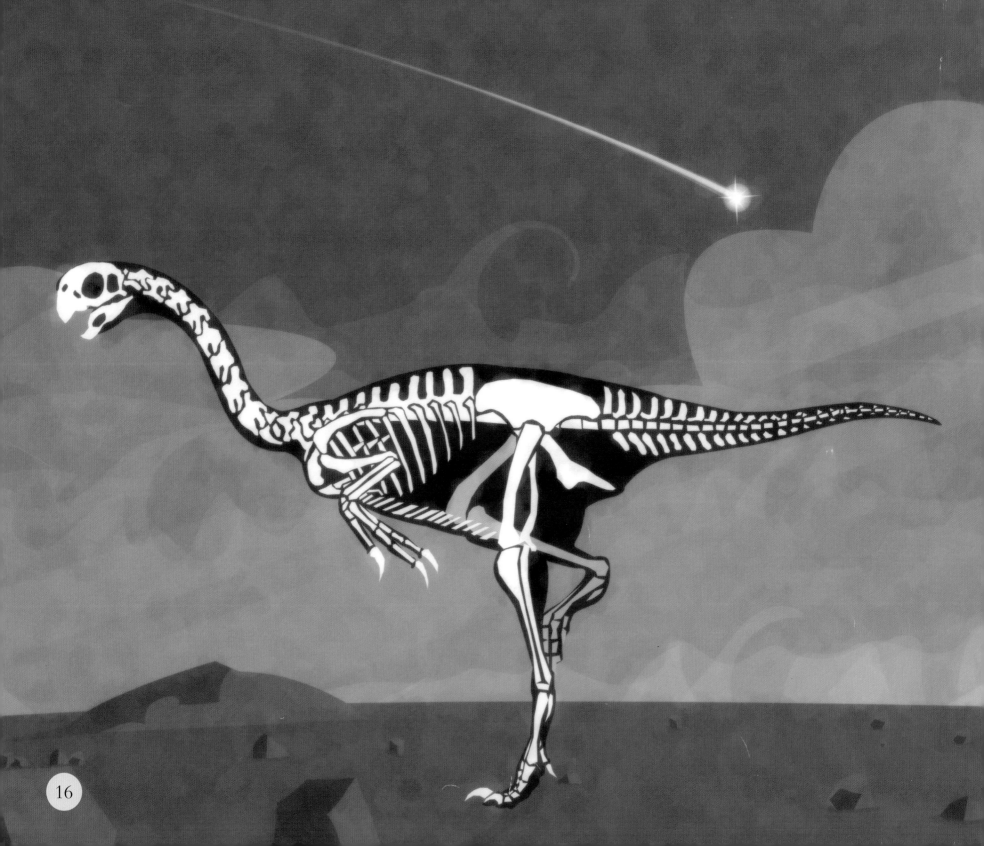

But dinosaurs have cousins that are hanging around.

You know the crocodile is just one that I've found.

Lots of different birds that fly around the tree.

Just look into the mirror maybe you or maybe me? No, we're not dinosaurs!

Way back 200 million years or more,
lots of things we can explore:
the sea, the sky, the stars, and more.

19

There's nothing cooler than a dinosaur.

Nothing cooler than a dinosaur.
Nothing cooler than a dinosaur.

GLOSSARY

extinct—no longer living; an extinct animal is one that has died out, with no more of its kind

herd—a large group of animals that lives or moves together

lava—the hot, liquid rock that pours out of a volcano when it erupts

paleontologist—scientist who studies prehistoric life

protection—to guard or keep safe from harm

squawk—to make a loud, harsh screech

Nothing Cooler Than a Dinosaur

Cody McKinney

Folk Rock

Online music access and CDs available at **www.cantatalearning.com**

23

ACTIVITY

Draw your own dinosaur! How big is your dinosaur? What does it eat? How many legs does it walk on! You get to decide when you create your own dinosaur.

TO LEARN MORE

Lessem, Don. *The Ultimate Dinopedia*. Washington, DC: National Geographic Children's Books, 2010.

Naish, Darren. *Dinosaurs Life Size*. Hauppauge, NY: Barrons Educational Series, Inc., 2010.

Olien, Rebecca. *How Do We Know about Dinosaurs?*: A Fossil Mystery. First Graphics. Mankato, MN: Capstone Press, 2012.

Throp, Claire. *Weekend with Dinosaurs*. Fantasy Field Trips. Chicago: Raintree, 2014.